_My First Book of_

# OPPOSITES

## Ruth Thomson • Illustrated by Chris McEwan

TREASURE PRESS

# day

# night

# dirty

# clean

# top

# bottom

# hot

# cold

# open

# shut

# wet

# dry

# up

# down

# big

# little

# fat

# thin

# soft

# hard

# push

# pull

# full

# empty

# noisy

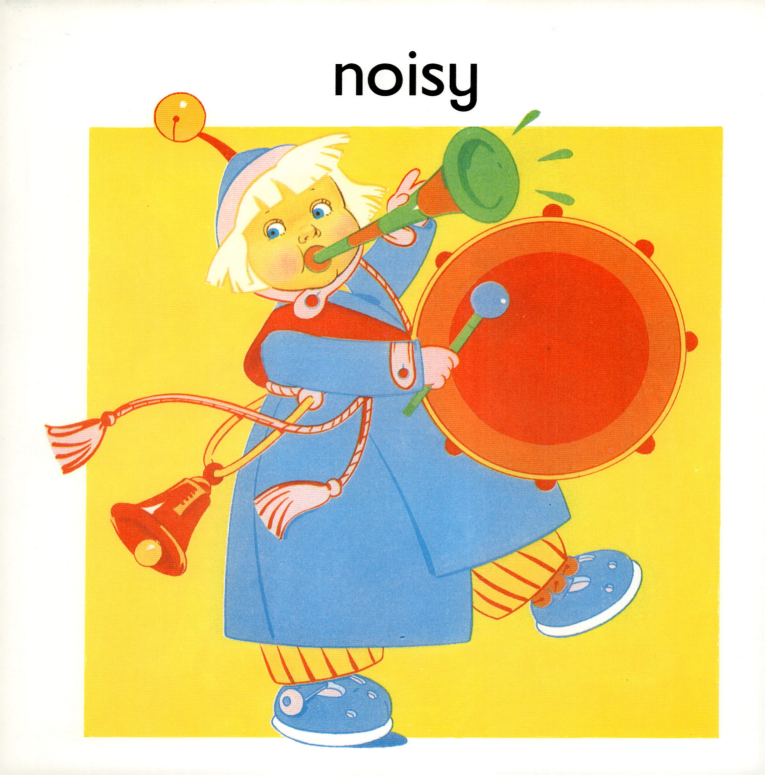

# quiet

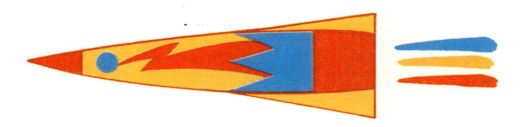

First published in Great Britain in 1986 by Conran Octopus Limited

This edition first published in Great Britain in 1990 by
Treasure Press
Michelin House
81 Fulham Road
London SW3 6RB

Designed by Heather Garioch
Educational consultant: Mark Evans, Lecturer in Education (Primary)
B.A. Hons, Oxon, P.G.C.E, Lond. M.Coll.P.

ISBN 1 85051 500 X

Printed in Great Britain